Contents

cards

HAWAII

People and Culture

Dorota Czarkowska Starzecka

Published for   The Trustees of the British Museum
by   British Museum Publications Limited

BM7 (STA)

Assistance freely given by my colleagues,
Mr B. A. L. Cranstone, and Miss E. M. Carmichael,
in preparing the text and illustrations is gratefully acknowledged.
The map was drawn by another colleague, Mr H. J. Gowers.

Designed by Dodd and Dodd
Set in 12/14 point Bembo
Printed in Great Britain
by Balding & Mansell, Wisbech and London

Introduction

The islands and the people

The Hawaiian islands lie in the north Pacific between lat. 18° 54′ and 28° 15′N and long. 154° 40′ and 178° 25′W, about 2000 miles from the west coast of North America. They consist of a long chain stretching diagonally from the north-west to the south-east across the Tropic of Cancer. The northern and central islands (the leeward islands) are small, almost uninhabited volcanic rocks and coral atolls. The eight main inhabited islands – Hawaii, Maui, Kahoolawe, Molokai, Lanai, Oahu, Kauai and Niihau – are situated at the southern end of the chain and are known as the windward islands. The whole group is part of a submarine mountain range created by volcanic eruptions over millions of years. The leeward end of the chain is almost completely eroded, with atolls built on the submerged mountain tops; the windward islands are volcanic mountains in various phases of development. There are remnants of fifteen volcanoes, some of them active. Mauna Loa (13,677ft) on Hawaii, erupting on an average every four and half years, is the world's largest active volcano, and Kilauea, also on Hawaii and almost continually active, is a great tourist attraction with its lake of molten lava, but volcanic activity is rarely a threat to life.

The climate is subtropical and conditioned by the north-east trade winds, which cause the windward side of the islands to be wet and cool. The leeward side escapes heavy rainfall and is warm and dry. Average day temperatures range from 74°–75°F in March to 79°–80°F in September. The windward sides, where not cultivated, are covered with forests, the leeward sides with grassland and scrub. There are cliffs on the coasts of most of the islands, but flat, sandy shorelines are usually found on the leeward side, and there are coral reefs, Hawaii being at the northern limit of coral distribution.

Flora and fauna are highly specialized, due to the isolation of the islands and great variations in environment within them. All the plants of greatest economic importance – taro, sweet potato, yam, breadfruit, bananas, sugar cane, gourds, bamboo and paper mulberry – were brought to the islands by the first settlers, as were also domesticated creatures – dogs, pigs and chickens. The only indigenous mammals, apart from whales and dolphins, were the monk seal and the hoary bat; there were no native reptiles or amphibians.

The islands were populated by Polynesians, a people originating ultimately in the region of south Asia, who spread through the Pacific over long periods, colonizing the islands of its eastern half. Exactly when the Polynesian immigrants arrived in Hawaii is not known, but by AD 500 the islands were already populated. The settlers came in several waves, initially probably from the Marquesas, and later from the Society Islands. In physical appearance they were tall, well-built, muscular, with a light brown skin, dark eyes and straight or wavy black hair.

Discovery and history

The first European discoverer of the Hawaiian group was Captain James Cook who arrived in the islands in 1778 during his third and last voyage. He named them 'the Sandwich Islands' in honour of the First Lord of the Admiralty. Captain Cook was favourably impressed by the Hawaiians, and they received him and his party with great hospitality and friendliness, paying particular deference to Cook himself whom they considered to be the god Lono (see p.20), whose return to the island had been predicted. With time, however, the constant needs of the ship's crew for supplies must have become a heavy burden on the local population, and the situation changed: friendliness was replaced by insolence and unpleasant incidents and misunderstandings culminated in a skirmish during which Captain Cook was killed.

At the time of Cook's visit the islands were divided into independent chiefdoms of feudal type, with a rigidly stratified society, a complex and tightly-

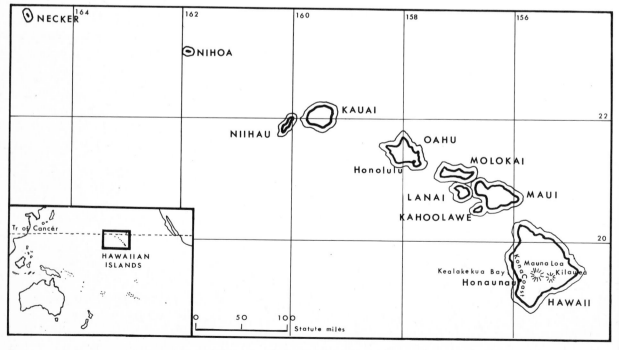

controlled political organization and an elaborate ceremonial and religious life (it is the culture of that period which is described further in this booklet).

Subsequent European contacts had a decisive influence on the development of Hawaiian society. By supplying firearms, they hastened the process of unification, which was achieved by King Kamehameha I ('the Great') in 1795, except for Kauai which submitted voluntarily in 1810. Ships engaged in the fur trade on the north-west coast of America visited Hawaii regularly, since it was a convenient revictualling and trading point. Trade increased when sandalwood was discovered in the islands but the supply was soon exhausted by indiscriminate exploitation. Whaling became of great economic importance, bringing about an increase in the numbers of foreign residents, particularly Americans. The sugar industry, concentrated in European hands, expanded and assumed vital economic importance when whaling declined; under such circumstances access to the American market became indispensable to the Hawaiian economy. The economic and political links with the United States grew closer and stronger.

Hawaiian history of that period is of a continuous diplomatic struggle to avoid annexation by foreign powers – Russia, France, Great Britain and the USA – and of the growth of American influence in the kingdom. This growth of the vested interests of the American residents was the main cause of the *coup d'état* of 1893 when the monarchy was deposed making way for annexation by the United States in 1898, Hawaii's strategic position in the Pacific being by then clear. Hawaii remained a Territory of the Union until 1959 when it was granted full statehood.

Western influences also shaped the social structure of Hawaii. King Kamehameha I maintained the traditional laws and religion but after his death in 1819 his son and successor Liholiho (Kamehameha II) abolished the old system, and the first missionaries arrived in 1820. In 1848 a land reform, known as the Great *Mahele* (or 'division'), was introduced by Kamehameha III; by it the land was divided among the people, preserving certain areas as Crown and government property. Four years later the first constitution was drafted and parliamentary government was established.

Simultaneously the population of the islands was changing drastically. The native Hawaiians, lacking resistance to foreign diseases and demoralized by the disintegration of the old system and values, declined in numbers and could not provide the labour force required by the sugar industry. This problem was solved by the importation of labour, starting in 1852 with the arrival of the first Chinese, soon followed by Japanese, Filipinos, Portuguese, Koreans and many others.

Today pure-blooded Hawaiians constitute only 1% of the population, the bulk of it consisting of Caucasians and Japanese. Virtually nothing remains alive of the old culture. Hawaii is a prosperous, modern state; its economy, relying mainly on agriculture (now expanding into other crops besides sugar cane and pineapple), the tourist trade and military expenditure (the headquarters

for all the US military operations in the Pacific are located in Hawaii), is growing steadily. But it is probably in the sphere of race relations that Hawaii has
been most successful; it is relatively free of racial problems and various ethnic
groups live harmoniously together, each contributing in its unique way to the
general pattern of life.

Hawaiian Society

Early Hawaiians

Very little is known about the culture of the first settlers of Hawaii. Archaeological evidence indicates a pattern of homesteads consisting of a few houses and occupied probably by an extended family group. Sacred places took the form of small platforms or enclosures. The main tool was a tanged stone adze of quadrangular cross-section, typical of Polynesia. The early inhabitants also manufactured bone fishhooks which today provide useful guidance in the relative dating of archaeological sites.

Particularly interesting and valuable evidence of Hawaiian culture as it existed in the fourteenth and fifteenth centuries is found on Nihoa and Necker, two small islands north-west of Kauai. They had already been abandoned at the time of the first European contacts, and the archaeological remains there were undisturbed. These include house sites and temples, agricultural terraces, fishhooks, adzes and stone vessels, as well as a particular type of stone image, found only on the island of Necker.

Petroglyphs, carved on rock surfaces throughout the islands, provide another insight into the culture of the early Hawaiians. Human figures, animals and artefacts are represented, and also numerous markings of unknown significance. Although the exact purpose of the petroglyphs is not clear, they seem to record events, commemorate legends and are probably connected with a desire to ensure personal well-being. The art of petroglyph carving was probably brought to the islands by the first immigrants and was continued well into the nineteenth century.

Social and political organization

At the time of the height of traditional Hawaiian culture, i.e. at the end of the eighteenth century, society was divided into four distinct castes: *ali'i* – chiefs and nobles; *kahuna* – priests and master-craftsmen; *maka'ainana* – commoners, cultivators, fishermen and craftsmen; *kauwa* – slaves and outcasts. It was governed according to the body of traditional and essentially religious laws known as the *kapu* system. *Kapu* is the Hawaiian equivalent of 'taboo' and means sacred or forbidden. It is one of the two main concepts of the Hawaiian philosophy of life, the basic one being that of *mana*. *Mana* is supernatural power which is the prerogative of gods but can be imparted to people and objects. Although potentially beneficial it is inherently dangerous. Since people – depending on their rank within the society and personal attributes – have it in varying degree, the *kapu* system was devised to regulate all social interaction by preventing danger which might result from free contacts between those with great *mana* and those with little or none.

The chiefs were ultimately descended from gods and thus were imbued with *mana* by virtue of their birth. *Mana* was linked to rank, and this was determined by genealogy. Rank was inherited in both paternal and maternal lines producing a cumulative effect. Marriages among the chiefs were arranged to produce offspring of the highest possible rank, which occasionally resulted in unions between brother and sister. Chiefs of the highest rank had so many restrictions connected with their *mana* that they were practically immobilized.

The *kahuna* included priests, master-craftsmen and experts in any particular field of knowledge. Among the priests the highest ranking were those serving Ku, the war god, followed by the priests of Lono, the god of peace and agriculture. Master-craftsmen and experts were not only highly skilled specialists, but also trained religious practitioners, possessing knowledge of religious rituals appropriate to their particular field. *Kahuna* specializing in sorcery were greatly feared, and people were aware of it as an ever-present danger. The training and duties of the *kahuna* were very exacting, and apprenticeship took many years.

The commoners constituted the bulk of the population. On them rested the burden of satisfying all the economic needs of the society; they were responsible for farming and fishing, and for construction works and their maintenance. They were free people, and if oppressed they could leave their district and settle under another chief. In times of war they were all called to arms and provided a body of fighting men.

The outcasts were landless, confined to special restricted areas and had no rights in the community. Their origins are not known but they might have been transgressors who broke the *kapu* or war prisoners, or perhaps descendants of the first wave of immigrants to the islands, overcome by the later settlers. They were polluting to everybody outside their caste, but they had a right of appeal to their chief in case of need. Their ranks supplied victims for human sacrifice when required.

Politically the islands were divided among independent supreme chiefs (*ali'i nui* or *moi*), who had special advisers: *kalaimoku*, responsible for the further division of the land among the minor chiefs, and *kahuna nui* – the high priest. The supreme chief ruled through the minor chiefs who, in turn, had executives (*konohiki*), whose duty it was to organize all the necessary work on the land and to collect taxes. Maintenance of law and order which meant, in effect, observing the *kapu* system, was the responsibility of constables (*ilamoku*).

Domestic life

There were no towns and no large settlements in Hawaii. People lived in scattered homesteads or small villages. An average homestead consisted of a number of separate houses. This was necessary because the *kapu* forbade men and women to eat and work together and domestic activities therefore had to be separated. There was the common sleeping house, the men's eating house where they kept their tools and weapons and which women were forbidden to enter, and the women's eating house. There was also a shed in which women made barkcloth and another to which they retired during periods of ritual uncleanliness. A farmer usually had a storehouse for the surplus of food, and those living by the sea had canoe sheds. A well-to-do household had a separate shrine where the household gods were kept and worshipped, but in more modest households the family altar was in the men's house.

The house itself was a thatched wood-frame structure, sometimes built on a stone platform, and had only one entrance and no windows. The floor might be covered with small pebbles, mats or dried grass. In cold regions the sleeping house had a fireplace in the middle of the floor. The house was built by the man with the help of his relatives. There was a consecrating ceremony before anyone was allowed to enter it, which consisted of the ceremonial cutting of the thatch over the doorway, performed by a *kahuna*.

Division of labour between the sexes was very clear-cut. Men were concerned with cultivation, fishing, the making of tools, utensils and weapons, house-building and religious ritual. Women cared for the children, helped in some agricultural tasks, collected wild foods, made barkcloth and plaited mats and baskets.

Cooking was a man's task and was done in earth ovens, separately for men and women. Stones were placed in a hole dug in the ground, and a fire was lit on them; when the stones were sufficiently hot, the remnants of the fire were removed and food, wrapped in leaves, was placed on the stones and covered with leaves, mats and earth to retain the heat. It took three to four hours to cook the food in this manner. As there was no pottery, boiling was done by dropping hot stones into wooden containers filled with water.

The staple food was *poi*, a thick paste made of pounded cooked taro mixed with water; there was also breadfruit, sweet potato and bananas. The *poi* was eaten by dipping fingers into the mixture and carrying it to the mouth; it could therefore, depending on its consistency, be described as 'one finger *poi*' or 'two finger *poi*'. *Poi* was the base of every meal and was served with fish and a relish of candle nuts, seaweed or salt. On special occasions pork was eaten and sometimes also dogs, but usually dogs were a food reserved for the chiefs. Some foods were forbidden to women by the *kapu*. All food was eaten cold.

Beverages consisted of water, coconut milk and '*awa* (kava), a mildly intoxicating drink often used in ceremonies and as an offering to the gods. Although in some regions of Polynesia kava drinking was accompanied by an elaborate ritual, in Hawaii it did not have such great ritual significance.

1 Objects of domestic use:
two stone *poi* pounders,
basalt breadfruit splitter,
hafted stone adze (2136;
1934. 12-5.24; 6280;
96-1151.)

The Hawaiians had no metals and their domestic implements were very simple, consisting mainly of shell scrapers and shredders, and bamboo and stone-flake knives. Wooden pounding boards and stone pounders were used for mashing taro (**1**), and food was served in wooden or gourd dishes (**2**).

The dress of the Hawaiians was simple and made of barkcloth (see p.31); men wore a loincloth (*malo*), women a knee-length skirt (*pa'u*), and both sexes wore a shawl or mantle (*kihei*) in cold weather. Chiefs and nobility wore ceremonial garments covered with feathers (**5, 6**). Personal ornaments, made of shells, seeds, ivory, feathers and animal teeth, were among the most refined in all Polynesia. The most spectacular ornament was a hook-shaped pendant called *lei niho palaoa*, carved from a sperm-whale tooth and suspended by two coils of finely braided human hair (**3**). It is probably a highly stylized representation of the head of a god; it was worn only by those of chiefly rank.

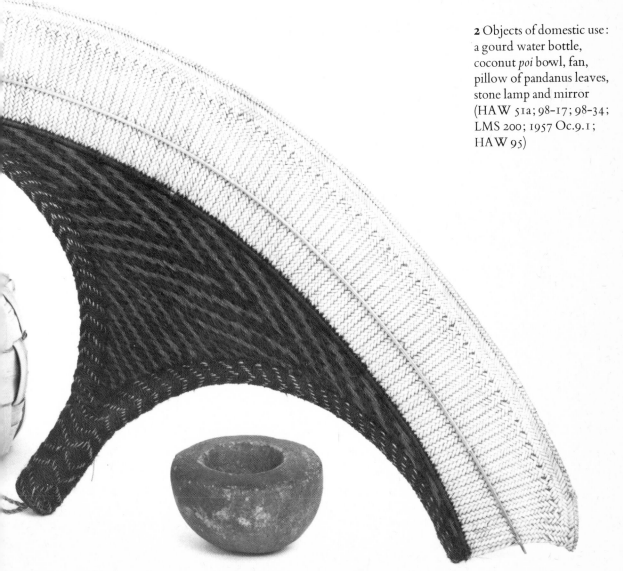

2 Objects of domestic use: a gourd water bottle, coconut *poi* bowl, fan, pillow of pandanus leaves, stone lamp and mirror (HAW 51a; 98-17; 98-34; LMS 200; 1957 Oc.9.1; HAW 95)

3 *Lei niho palaoa*, a necklace of sperm-whale ivory, suspended by coils of braided human hair (54.12-23.11)

The most valued possession of women were necklaces (*lei*) made of feathers, which were also worn as head-bands. Bracelets were made of boar's tusks or closely fitting plates of turtle shell and bone strung together (**4**). Ivory ornaments carved into various shapes were worn on the wrist or as rings. Anklets of dog's teeth, shells or seeds were worn when dancing.

People frequently adorned themselves with fragrant leaves and flowers. Tattooing was practised but was not very elaborate, consisting of geometric designs and pictographs. Candle nut or sugar cane charcoal was used as pigment. Acrid vegetable juices painted on the body temporarily produced the effect of tattooing.

Medicine was relatively highly developed. It was practised by the *kahuna* and consisted of herb remedies, massage, steam baths, poultices as well as various forms of psychotherapy.

The Hawaiians had no medium of exchange, no 'money', and there were no markets. Although food and goods were continually exchanged between members of the kin group (*ohana*), it was done informally. Trade existed only in the localities where there was a considerable surplus of goods. The Hawaiians disapproved of commercialism and favoured sharing and cooperation. Accumulation of wealth existed only among the nobility, but its importance as a status symbol precluded any trading.

4 Bracelets of boars' tusks, and one of turtle shell and bone plates (HAW 151, 156 and 157)

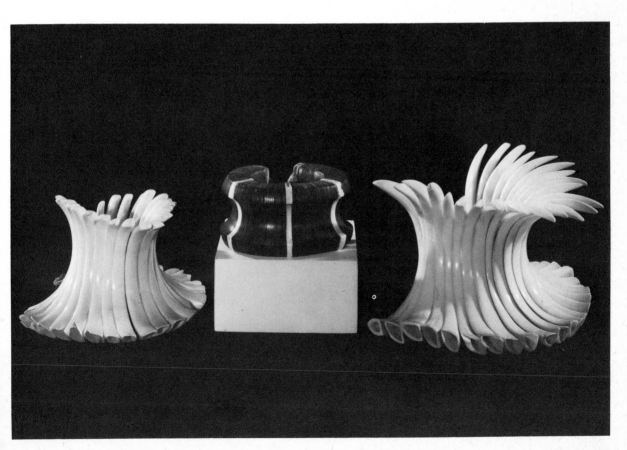

Religion

The gods

Religion was the most important aspect of Hawaiian life. It permeated every sphere and no event of any significance took place without associated religious ritual. Every major event in the life of an individual – birth, marriage or death, every major practical undertaking – building a house or a canoe, the whole agricultural cycle and everything connected with fishing – all were accompanied by the appropriate religious ceremonies, as were all the regular calendrical celebrations the aim of which was to ensure the prosperity and well-being of the people.

The Hawaiians worshipped innumerable deities of various orders of importance. They had a concept of the supreme and absolute god but all knowledge of this deity was esoteric, restricted to a small group of the initiated priests, and virtually nothing is known about it today. The population at large was familiar with two main categories of gods: *akua* – cosmic deities representing nature's elements, and *'aumakua* – familiar, protective gods, very often deified ancestors.

The four cosmic deities were Kane, the creator of nature and men, god of sunlight and fresh water, concerned with life and procreation; Kanaloa, who was associated with Kane but of relatively little importance in the Hawaiian pantheon; Ku, the most aggressive and active of the gods, who was the god of war and a special god of the chiefs (**11, 14**); and finally Lono, the god of rain and agriculture, who was also the most benevolent and humane, concerned with forgiveness and healing.

The *akua* had numerous manifestations emphasizing their various aspects – Ku, for example, could be Ku-of-war, Ku-of-fishing, Ku-adzing-out-the-canoe, and Ku-the-snatcher-of-islands. In such form they were patrons of various crafts and activities.

'Aumakua were worshipped in household shrines and they provided protection and were the source of emotional security to the common people. There were also numerous other gods, demi-gods and culture heroes, among them

5 Feather capes (Royal Loan; NN)

16

Pele, the goddess of volcanoes, Laka, patron of the dance, and Maui, the trick-ster who was credited with having fished the islands out of the sea. Women worshipped their own deities, particularly Hina, a goddess associated with the moon. Very important among the supernatural beings were evil spirits, usually souls who did not reach the land of the dead, and whom sorcerers could coerce into service. A very special place in Hawaiian mythology is given to little people, of whom Menehune were the most popular. Menehune were two to three feet high, ugly, but muscular and strong, and they helped people by building temples and fishponds. They were shy and worked only at night; in their free time they were full of joy and mischief, fond of games and sports.

Temples and rituals

The great gap existing in Hawaiian society between the nobility and the com-moners was also reflected in the religious rituals performed by the two groups. The commoners worshipped their familiar 'aumakua in household shrines or special patron gods at occupational shrines, whereas the chiefs presided at pro-longed and spectacular ceremonies devoted to the akua and conducted by priests in open-air temples called heiau. Heiau, which could be built only at the order of a chief, were of two main types: one, called luakini, in which human sacrifices were offered, was dedicated to Ku; the other, mapele, was dedicated to Lono, and offerings consisted of pigs, vegetable foods and barkcloth. Apart from minor differences in the furnishings of the temples resulting from their different functions, a heiau was a rectangular court, sometimes built in terraces, surrounded with stone walls or wooden fences. Inside there was a raised plat-form on which stood the oracle tower entered by priests to receive messages from the gods, temple houses for the high chief and priest, buildings for storing temple drums, an offering stand, a refuse pit for decayed offerings, and finally a number of large wooden images of gods.

In any religious ritual the absolute perfection of its execution was of the ut-most importance for it was the only guarantee of its effectiveness. This mechan-istic approach to worship had wider implications in Hawaiian religion for the emphasis was not on a moral code but on securing favours of the gods for one's own advantage through the correct ritual.

The most important of the religious ceremonies, involving the whole popu-lation, was the annual celebration of *Makahiki*. This was the harvest festival devoted to Lono, lasting from October to February, and signalled by the appearance of the constellation Pleiades. During this festival war was forbidden and taxes were collected. The first period of the *Makahiki* was the *kapu* time, when people stopped working and brought their offerings to special altars set up at district boundaries. The image of Lono, symbolized by a long pole with a crosspiece to which two large sheets of white barkcloth were attached, was paraded round the island, accompanied by the high chief and priests, acknow-ledging the offerings at the altars. When the circuit was completed, the *kapu* was lifted and the second period of the celebrations followed, the time of play,

6 Feather cloak (NN)
7 Helmets, two covered with feathers and one of plain basketry (HAW 107 and 108; VAN 237)

feasting and general enjoyment. Captain Cook visited the islands during the *Makahiki* celebrations and was received by the Hawaiians as Lono – the similarity between the image of Lono and the ship's sails was striking. His death may have had some connection with the ritual mock spearing of Lono as represented by the high chief at the conclusion of the festivities to signal the end of peace, and with the growing suspicion and disappointment among the Hawaiians that Cook was, after all, human. During the *Makahiki* celebrations the *hula* ceremony was performed. The *hula*, now a tourist attraction, was a sacred dance performed in honour of gods and of chiefs who were descendants of gods. In preparation for the ceremony, musicians and dancers spent weeks in seclusion, under strict *kapu*, in a house specially built for the purpose, where they practised their singing and dancing. Public performance was preceded by a consecration of the performers and ceremonial sacrifice of a pig.

The Food Quest

System of land tenure

The system of land holding and its use was feudal. The supreme chief had the right to dispose of the land which he held in trust for the gods. He did so by distributing it among the high chiefs, reserving some portion for his own use. The high chiefs in turn distributed the land among the minor chiefs, warriors and supervising agents who allotted it to the commoners who cultivated it. The land holdings of the chiefs were neither permanent nor hereditary for a chief's accession to power was followed by re-apportioning the land among his followers. This did not, however, affect the commoners; they were usually secure in their tenancy for it was to the advantage of the chiefs to have the land cultivated in peace and thus be assured of a constant and regular supply of necessary produce.

Each large island, or *mokupui*, ruled by a supreme chief, was divided into smaller districts called *moku*; these were usually wedge-shaped, the lines of division running from the top of the mountains to the sea. Each *moku* was then divided into *ahupua'a*, which were tax collecting units. It was at the altars set up at the boundaries of *ahupua'a* that the taxes were paid in kind during the *Makahiki* season. *Ahupua'a* were subdivided into *'ili* which belonged to the tenant farmers.

The last redistribution of land took place during the reign of King Kamehameha I when he finally united the islands. His successor, Kamehameha II, did not follow the old custom of land reallotment, and Kamehameha III introduced the Great *Mehele*. As a result roughly one third of all the land became Crown Lands, one third was the property of the chiefs and the remaining third was claimed by tenant farmers as their *kuleana*. The king and the chiefs relinquished portions of their holdings to create government land.

Agriculture

The main cultivated food plants were taro, sweet potato, breadfruit, yam, banana, coconut, arrowroot, sugar cane and *'awa* (kava, *Piper methysticum*). Of

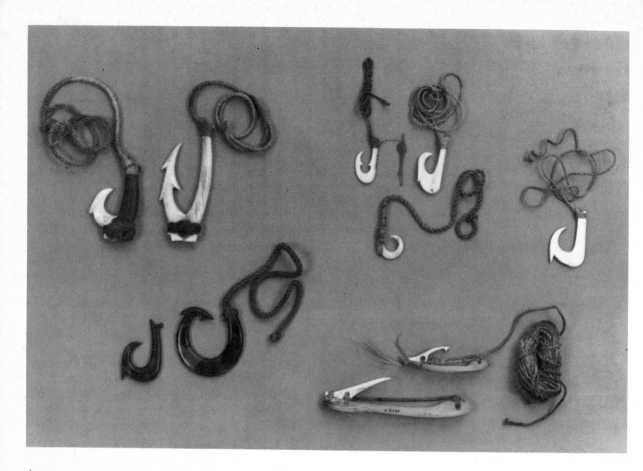

8 Various kinds of fish hooks: composite; simple, of bone, pearl shell or turtle shell, and trolling hooks (HAW 65; 1944 Oc.2.69; VAN 330; HAW 73; NN; 1944 Oc.2.73 and 74; HAW 377; 1944 Oc.2.71)

these taro was the most important and most widely cultivated; in dry areas unsuitable for taro, sweet potato was the principal crop.

The only cultivating tool used was a digging stick, made of hard wood, with a pointed or spatulate end. Digging sticks which had been used successfully for a length of time were thought to have special powers and were family treasures.

Farming was essentially a male occupation but women shared in some agricultural tasks, particularly in the coastal areas where men spent most of their time fishing. Women could cultivate sweet potato and other plants but never taro; every aspect of taro economy was exclusively men's work. Taro (*Colocasia esculenta*) is a plant with heart-shaped leaves and an edible starchy tuberous root, propagated by planting side shoots or tops of the tubers. In the uplands, in high rainfall localities dry taro was grown, often with a mulch of rotted leaves. Wet taro was sometimes planted along streams and in swamps but the preferred method of cultivation – whenever terrain and water supply permitted – was on artificially built terraces with retaining walls of earth and stone, irrigated from streams by means of skilfully constructed systems of channels.

Besides the food plants, many others were cultivated. Among them were pandanus, the leaves of which were used for mat plaiting; bamboo, which produced material for tools, containers, musical instruments and irrigation pipes; paper mulberry, the bark of which was used for barkcloth manufacture; gourds, for making vessels; *ti* (*Cordyline terminalis*), the leaves used for wrapping and also as food; *olona* (*Touchardia latifolia*), the fibre of which provided material for cordage; turmeric, for dye; candle nut (*Aleurites moluccana*), which provided oil, for lighting and for food.

Although cultivation was practised universally in Polynesia, it was only in Hawaii that – owing to the difficult terrain and seasonal variations of the climate – it became a thoroughly systematic, highly skilled occupation and led to the development of a true peasantry. This had cultural implications: during the harvest time war was prohibited, and in certain ways farming took precedence over other occupations for every male child was consecrated to Lono, god of agriculture and peace. Farming was not just a means of making a living but a complete way of life. Religious beliefs were an integral part of it and every stage of cultivation was accompanied by the appropriate religious ritual.

Fishing and canoes

Fishing played an extremely important part in the economy for next to *poi*, fish was the staple food of the Hawaiians. It was a remarkably skilled occupation, held in high esteem, and demanding extensive training. There was competition among fishermen and knowledge acquired by successive generations was jealously guarded. Like any other activity of significance, fishing had its gods and prescribed ritual. On the water's edge there were fishing shrines consisting of heaps of stones to which fishermen going out to fish contributed by adding one.

Methods of fishing were varied: catching by hand, spearing, netting, trapping, noosing and hook and line fishing were all used.

Catching by hand was practised in shallow waters, in holes and rock crevices. Fishing spears were of plain hard wood, slender, sharply pointed and tapering at the butt end. Nets, usually made of *olona* fibre, were of various shapes and sizes: scoop nets attached to a frame of pliable wood bent in a curve, the ends brought together; two-handled scoop nets with two parallel sticks instead of a curved frame; rectangular dip nets tied at the corners to the ends of two curved rods crossed at right angles and suspended from a line attached where they crossed; bag-nets into which fish were driven and the net closed by pulling a cord threaded through the meshes around the opening; and seine nets with wooden floats and stone sinkers. Basketry traps – hemispherical, cylindrical and funnel-shaped – were also used. Fishhooks were adapted for catching different kinds of fish and had a wide range of shapes and sizes (**8**). They were made of bone, shell, turtle shell or wood, with or without barbs, either in one piece or with separate point and shank lashed together. Each hook had a snood, a short length of cord bound permanently to the shank, for quick attachment to a fishing line. Fish-hooks made of human bone were particularly valued since they were supposed to have *mana*. Trolling hooks used in bonito fishing had a shank of pearl shell, the point was almost always made of human bone, and a few pig bristles were attached to the point end. Large wooden hooks with bone points were used to

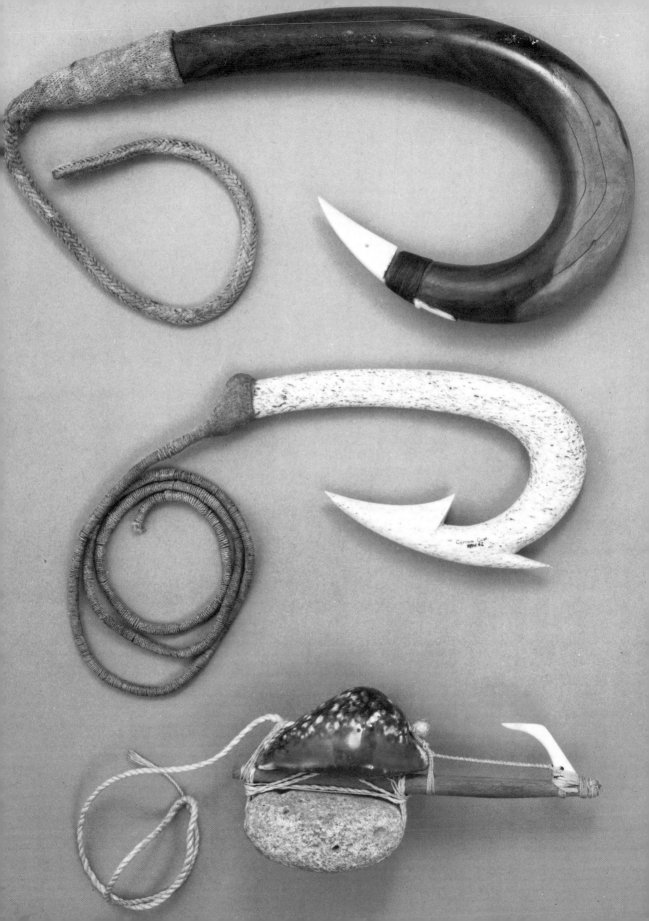

catch sharks (**9**), human flesh was used as a bait when the chiefs went fishing. The hooks were shaped by binding a shoot so that it grew in a curve. Sharks were also caught using a slip noose. Squid were caught with a lure consisting of a cowrie shell and a stone sinker lashed to a hook (**9**), or by spearing. Both shark and squid fishing were sports of the chiefs, and fishing by torch light at night was very popular.

Fishing grounds were preserved by imposing *kapu* on them during certain times of the year. Fish were also raised in a systematic way in special tidal ponds built offshore.

The most essential part of a fisherman's equipment was a canoe. Canoes were also the only means of transport between the islands and they were used in war. There were two types of canoe, the single outrigger and the double canoe. The outrigger was usually between 15 and 24ft long, the double canoe could be over 70ft long, but both were constructed in a similar way: a dugout hull made from a single tree trunk was fitted with washstrakes to raise the sides, bow and stern end pieces and U-shaped spreaders inside the hull to which the booms were attached. Double canoes had two parallel hulls of equal length, when the available logs permitted, fixed the required distance apart by curved cross booms on which a platform for passengers and cargo was built. The outrigger had two booms, the float was curved, and its ends clear of the water. Sail was optional for the outrigger but double canoes were always equipped to carry it. The sail, made of matting, was triangular with the apex downwards, and the usual mode of propulsion was by paddling.

The Hawaiians did not decorate their canoes except by painting the hull black and giving it a gloss by dressing it with candle nut oil. Fishing canoes carried spear racks, some of which were carved, lashed to the booms.

9 A squid lure and two shark hooks, one of bone, the other of wood with a bone point (98-29; HAW 62; NN)

Warfare

Weapons

Wars were frequent. There was constant rivalry among the supreme chiefs who either wanted to enlarge their domains by conquest, or were forced to defend their position against ambitious usurpers, eager to increase their status by victory.

There was no standing army but a high chief kept at his court a small body of professional warriors called *koa*. They spent their time practising their skills in warlike exercises and mock battles. The chiefs were trained from early childhood in the use of various weapons and were always accomplished fighters. Captain Vancouver in his *Voyage of discovery* . . . , (London 1798, vol. 2, pp. 151–2) described King Kamehameha I taking part in a war game: '. . . and defended himself with the greatest dexterity, much to our surprise and admiration; in one instance particularly, against six spears that were hurled at him nearly at the same instant; three he caught as they were flying, with one hand, two he broke by parrying them with his spear in the other, and the sixth by a trifling inclination of his body, passed harmless'. The rest of the population received no formal training in the use of weapons.

Weapons included spears, daggers, clubs, shark-toothed weapons, slings and tripping weapons (**13**). Spears were made of wood, in one piece, and ranged in length from 6 to 18ft. The short ones were often barbed and were used both for thrusting and throwing; the long ones were plain, thickened at the butt end and were used as pikes. Wooden daggers had a sharply pointed double-edged blade or resembled the cut-off top end of a long spear, both types being perforated for a wrist-cord attachment. Clubs were made either of wood or stone, or had a stone head lashed to a wooden handle, and they also had a wrist cord at the butt end. Some had a long, sharp butt end and could also be used as daggers.

Shark-tooth weapons were shaped like flat clubs with the teeth pegged or lashed round the edges. Wood and cord knuckledusters set with shark teeth were also used. Tripping weapons consisted of weights of wood or stone to which a cord was attached; sometimes they were provided with handles and resembled clubs.

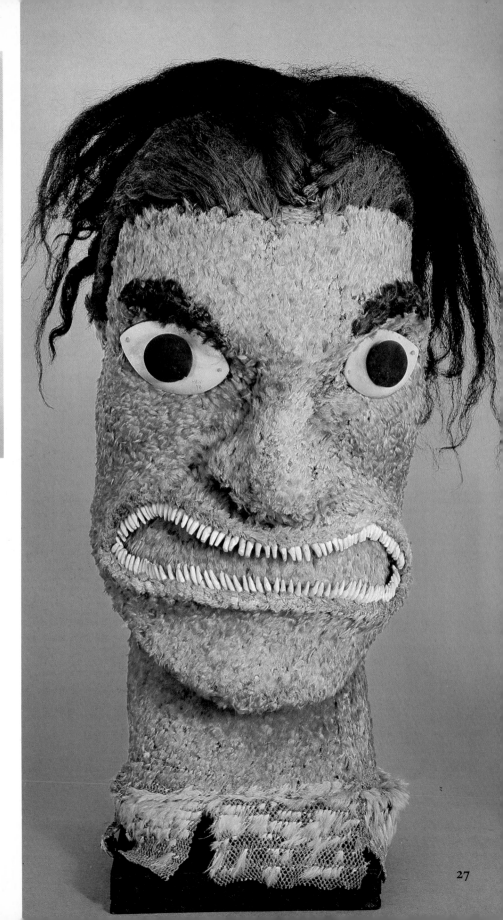

10 Feather image,
probably representing the
war god Ku (HAW 78)
11 Feather image,
probably of the war god
Ku (LMS 221)

12 Temple image in Kona style (LMS 223)

13 Weapons: four shark-tooth weapons, a stone-headed club, wooden tripping weapon, and two daggers, one of wood, the other of sawfish bone (VAN 264; HAW 188 and 187; 2043; VAN 266; HAW 178 and 182; 9059)

Slings were made of plaited vegetable fibre and specially shaped ovoid stones were used with them. In naval battles canoe breakers were used; these were heavy stones with an encircling deep groove for a rope; they were hurled at the enemy canoes and retrieved by the rope.

The bow, although known in Hawaii and used in sport, was never treated as a weapon.

Methods of warfare

Warfare was formalized and religious ritual played a major role in it. Before a war was declared, the gods were consulted and sacrifices were made to the war god Ku. Only after the priests pronounced the omens favourable were messengers sent over the country to call men to arms. They arrived with their weapons and provisions, often accompanied by their wives who came to be on hand in case their men were wounded; some of them also fought at the side of their husbands. Old people, children and the rest of the women withdrew for protection to mountain fortresses or special places of refuge.

Battles were fought in daylight, in open country, in a straightforward and well-regulated manner. The preferred method of fighting was hand-to-hand combat and the battle progressed with this end in view. At the start, when the armies advanced upon each other, warriors used slings and short throwing spears, but in direct hand-to-hand fighting they changed to daggers, clubs and shark-tooth weapons. The long spear was very popular as an all-purpose weapon. In pursuit tripping weapons were used.

The chief's station was in the centre of his army, accompanied by priests carrying portable images of the gods and encouraging the warriors. The professional warriors, *koa*, acted as the champions and often engaged in single combat while both armies watched awaiting the outcome.

The vanquished were pursued and cut down without mercy, sometimes for days and weeks after the battle was over, and their country was divided among the victors. Fugitives who reached a place of refuge were saved. Sometimes a warrior of the conquered army might plead for mercy with the victorious chief, but if he were spared it was only to be made a slave or to be saved for a future human sacrifice.

The victorious side buried their dead but those of the enemy were left to rot or to be devoured by dogs and pigs.

Victory was celebrated with religious ceremonies during which human sacrifices were offered in the temples. If a peace treaty was agreed upon, it was ratified in the temple. Finally, feasting, dancing and public games followed when the common people celebrated the end of the war.

Arts and Crafts

Barkcloth

The Hawaiians were skilled craftsmen and any product of their workmanship – be it a canoe, an adze or a fish-hook – was carefully finished, functional and effective, but in some fields their achievement was truly outstanding. The most striking examples are barkcloth, featherwork and wood carving. Hawaiian barkcloth, *kapa*, was undoubtedly the best produced in Oceania. It was manufactured mainly from the paper mulberry (*Broussonetia papyrifera*). The saplings were cut when they reached a height of 6–12ft, and the bark was stripped. The outer layer was peeled off and discarded, and the inner bark was soaked in bowls of sea water for about a week to make it soft and pliable. It was then beaten with a round wood beater on a stone anvil into standard-sized rough sheets which were dried and bleached in the sun and stored to await the second stage of beating. This was preceded by soaking the barkcloth in water again and beating was done with quadrangular beaters on wooden anvils in special houses set aside for this purpose. The wooden anvils were hollow underneath and when set up on two stones, were highly resonant; it was said that women could convey messages when beating *kapa* and were able to recognize the sound of their own anvils. The beating progressed from using the most coarsely grooved side of the beater first to the finest last. Large pieces of cloth were made by overlapping smaller pieces and felting them together. When the cloth was finished a design was impressed on it with one of the beater's surfaces to form a 'watermark' and the process was completed by beating the cloth with the smooth surface of the beater. Some cloth was further treated to produce a ribbed effect: the damp cloth was placed over a grooved board or anvil, and with a special implement held alongside a bamboo ruler, it was forced into the grooves underneath.

The range of colours, mineral or vegetable, used in decorating barkcloth was wider than anywhere else in Polynesia. Methods of decorating included overlaying, cord snapping, freehand painting and printing. Overlaying was done by beating together a coloured piece of cloth placed over a plain one. In cord snapping a cord, dipped in dye, was stretched over the cloth, lifted in the middle and allowed to snap back, which produced a coloured line showing the twist of the cord. Painting executed with the help of bamboo and wood liners and rulers was widely practised when Captain Cook visited the islands, but shortly afterwards the printing technique was developed. The stamps were lengths of bamboo with a pattern carved at one end and printing was done by dipping the stamp in dye and pressing it against the cloth. By continuous stamping in rows and using different stamps, a great variety of patterns could be produced.

Barkcloth was often scented. This was done either by adding scent to the dye, or by placing fragrant plants between the sheets of cloth. Barkcloth was used primarily for clothing, each type of garment requiring a special kind of cloth. Bed-covers were made by sewing together along one side a number of large sheets, the top one of which was decorated; the thickness of the cover could be altered by turning the layers back. Barkcloth was also used for floor covering, in burials, and as wicks in oil lamps, and it had ceremonial uses: white cloth was used to wrap the images of gods and to cover the oracle towers in the temples.

Featherwork

Featherwork can be divided into two categories of objects: chiefly regalia, consisting of capes (**5**), cloaks (**6**), helmets (**7**) and feathered staffs of state (**10, 11**), and images of gods. Except in the case of staffs, the technique in both, however, was essentially the same, the main difference being that on images and helmets the featherwork was supported on a basketry frame. The feather capes, cloaks and helmets were ceremonial garments of the nobility, symbolizing their elevated social status. They were worn on ceremonial occasions and in battle, and were forbidden to commoners and women. The capes and cloaks were called 'ahu'ula which means 'red garments'. Red was the colour associated with gods and chiefs throughout Polynesia, but in Hawaii yellow replaced red as the chiefly colour owing to the greater scarcity value of yellow feathers.

The yellow feathers were obtained from birds called 'o'o (*Moho nobilis*) and *mamo* (*Drepanis pacifica*); the red from 'i'iwi (*Vestiaria coccinea*) and *apapane* (*Himatione sanguinea*). The birds were caught in the moulting season by professional hunters, with bird lime, nets or snares, and were usually released after plucking, unless this was so drastic that the birds could not survive, in which case they were killed and eaten. Domestic fowl, the tropic bird and the man-of-war hawk provided feathers for inferior capes of minor chiefs; cloaks were worn only by the high chiefs. Both capes (**5**) and cloaks (**6**) have a netting foundation made of *olona* fibre cord, often consisting of several pieces cut to shape and joined together. The feathers are tied in small bundles to the net meshes, starting from the lower border, each successive row of feathers hiding the quills of the row below. The upper and side edges of the netting are bound with a square braid of *olona*.

Although feather garments were made also in Tahiti and New Zealand, the

Hawaiian technique is a local development and may have derived from *ti*-leaf rain capes where the leaves were attached to a fishing net base.

The most common colour scheme was a red background with yellow geometrical motifs and yellow lower border. The motifs were crescents, lozenges, triangles and occasionally discs. The side edges were decorated with half-motifs, each pair forming a complete design when brought together. The most valuable cloaks and capes were those with a yellow background. The capes showed a greater variety of decorative patterns than the cloaks – black was often used, although sparingly – but the overall design was always fairly simple, well-defined and restrained.

Helmets (*mahiole*) were made of split aerial roots of '*ie'ie* (*Freycinetia arborea*), inter-plaited at right angles (**7**). The feathers were attached by being tied either to the netting which was fitted over the helmet, or to one side of a three-ply braid, which was fastened to the helmet in successive layers. The helmets of the high chiefs were always covered with feathers; those of the minor chiefs and warriors were often left plain.

The chiefly regalia were completed by feathered staffs of state called *kahili*. The handle was made of wood or of discs of turtle shell, bone or ivory strung on a slender rod and fitting closely together; sometimes human bone was used, to honour the deceased. For the tops of *kahili* a variety of feathers was used.

To describe the effect which those spectacular chiefly regalia must have created it is best to let an eye-witness speak. C. S. Stewart, a sympathetic and sensitive missionary in the islands in the years 1823–25, wrote in his *Journal of a residence in the Sandwich Islands . . .* (London, 1828, pp. 117–18): 'I doubt whether there is a nation in Christendom, which at the time letters and Christianity were introduced, could have presented a *court dress* and insignia of rank so magnificent as those: and they were found here in all their richness, when the islands were discovered by Cook. There is something approaching the *sublime* in the lofty noddings of the kahiles of state, as they tower far above the heads of the group whose distinction they proclaim: something conveying to the mind impressions of greater majesty than the gleamings of the most splendid banner I ever saw unfurled'.

The feather images of gods are unique to Hawaii. They were portable personal gods of the high chiefs. As they were carried into battle, they probably represent the war god Ku (**10, 11**).

It seems likely that the images may have evolved from the feather helmets, for the principle of their construction is basically the same: a basketry frame covered with netting to which feathers are attached. Some images were adorned with a crest, others had human hair attached; all had pearl-shell eyes with wooden pegs forming pupils and holding the eyes in position, and teeth, for which dogs' teeth were used. The feathers were the same as those used in cloaks and helmets. The predominant colour was red, with yellow and some black on the crest. Black feathers were also used for the eyebrows.

Wood carving

Wood carving skills found expression in the manufacture of purely utilitarian objects like food bowls, and in sculpture.

Bowls are among the most attractive of Hawaiian artefacts. They have very elegant simple lines and a beautiful finish. They were never decorated with surface carving (gourd containers on the other hand were frequently decorated with geometrical patterns by incising a design on the surface, removing the outer skin between the decorative motifs and immersing the vessel in a swamp which darkened the exposed surface).

In carving a bowl the outer contours were shaped first and then the inside was hollowed out using an adze or a chisel; when the wood was difficult to work, carefully controlled fire was used to remove the core. The bowl was then soaked in the sea for a week and afterwards kept filled with food, changed every few days, until the bitter taste of the wood was removed. Finally it was smoothed with pumice and polished with green bamboo leaves and candle nut oil.

Bowls were transported in especially made nets (**14**), with a carrying pole in

16 Two-tone bowl for *poi* with human figure supports (HAW 47)

the case of large bowls. Some bowls with covers, often very large, were used for storing food, fishing gear, barkcloth and feather garments. Shallow dishes and platters were used for serving meat. Superior bowls, probably reserved for the chiefs, had carved human figure supports (**15–17**). A specialized form was the finger bowl, for washing hands after meals; such bowls have an external handle and an internal flange for scraping any fat or sticky substance off the fingers (**14**). For the chiefs very special bowls were made into which they deposited remnants of their meals; these were later destroyed to prevent any possibility of their use for sorcery. Some of these bowls were inlaid with the teeth of dead enemies as a gesture of final insult (**14**). Bowls were treasured and when broken were carefully repaired with small pieces of wood driven across the broken edges.

Wood sculpture, mainly images of gods, represents the highest artistic achievement of the Hawaiians. The images are powerful, aloof, with a strong sense of potential vitality and aggression. They were carved by priest-craftsmen, skilled in both wood carving and religious ritual. The task of carving was a sacred rite, an attempt to transform abstract concepts into concrete forms. The images themselves were not sacred, they only became so when gods were induced to enter them.

The religious images can be divided into three categories: temple images, stick images and free-standing images.

Temple images are monumental in scale and threatening in expression. Among the most distinctive are those in Kona style (from the Kona coast of

17 Double bowl for relish (HAW 48)

18 Stick images of gods (HAW 174)

19 Image of a deity with
pearl-shell eyes (1944
Oc.2.716)

Hawaii where the style developed), characterized by the elaboration of the hair
with its two downward sweeps, a figure-of-eight mouth, extended nostrils, and
eyes located off the face and in the hair, following its curve (**12**). The central
image in the temple was the most elaborately carved and the ceremony of its
setting up was marked with a human sacrifice.

Stick images are small, portable images with shafts, from 3 to 24in. in length
(**18**). They show a great variety of styles and a concern for refinement and
finish. These images, although owned privately, were also used during ceremonies in the temples.

Free-standing images tend to be bigger than the stick images, and show a certain realism. Some of them have pearl-shell eyes, human teeth and human hair
pegged in (**19**). This group includes the sorcery images, usually the ones with
hollowed-out backs.

There is one group of images, quite different in character from the images of
gods. These are the human supports for bowls, drums etc., mentioned above (**20**).
These carvings were entirely secular, and so they are informal, very often

20 Image of a deity for
supporting bowls or
drums (1657)

carved in acrobatic postures, and there is a certain air of playfulness about them. From the point of view of composition they are very ingeniously integrated into the object, often being vital to its function.

The tools used in carving were stone adzes, gouges and chisels, sharp chips of volcanic glass, and shark-tooth gravers. The pump drill was used for drilling holes. Porous stones, coral, ray and shark skin and sand were used for smoothing. Polishing was done by rubbing with charcoal, then with bamboo and bread-fruit leaves, and finally with barkcloth. Varnish was provided by the application of candle nut oil. In rare cases pigment was used – sparingly – to decorate images.

Hawaiian sculpture shows many characteristics of style in common with other Polynesian art styles but some traits are distinctively Hawaiian. These are fully developed three-dimensional forms with parts of the body as separate units, conveying a sense of poised vitality, the elaboration of the head, a protruding jaw–mouth–tongue complex, eye dislocation in Kona images, and the use of supplementary materials for eyes, hair and teeth.

Pastimes

Games

The Hawaiians were a gregarious, fun-loving people and they spent a great deal of their time in games, sports, singing and dancing.

The popular games of the Hawaiians included *no'a*, in which one group of players hid an object under one of several bundles of barkcloth and the other group had to guess which; *puhenehene*, in which the object was concealed on the person of one of the players; *konane*, a variety of checkers played on a wood board with black and white pebbles; *maika*, in which stone discs were thrown or bowled between two sticks set in the ground, and *pahe'e* and *moa*, both contests in dart or javelin throwing. There were also various courtship games, different versions of which were played by the commoners and the chiefs.

Boxing, wrestling and racing were very popular. Sledging was an aristocratic pastime: wooden sleds were used to slide down hillsides on tracks built of stone and earth. The greatest Hawaiian sport, however, was surfing. Surf boards could be short, 6–9ft in length, or long, about 15ft. They were carefully carved and smoothed, and were stained dark and polished with candle nut oil. Expert riders could ride the surf kneeling or standing on the boards, and still do in this popular pastime.

Music, dance and poetry

Music, dance and poetry were all linked together and had a deeper, religious significance. This was best expressed in the *hula*, in which the dancing was accompanied by chanting and drumming. Drums were probably the most important musical instrument. Small, wooden drums were used in the *hula*, the tall ones were used in temples. Gourd drums, made of two gourds joined together one above the other, and knee drums of coconut shell, so called because they were tied to the player's leg above the knee, were also used in the *hula*.

Other musical instruments included gourd and bamboo rattles, nose flutes, jew's harps, small gourd nose whistles called lovers' whistles, shell trumpets and musical bows.

One of the favourite pastimes was listening to the chanting of *mele* or poetical songs. Composers of *mele* were highly respected because their art demanded great erudition. A *mele* had many levels of meaning: the apparent meaning, the crude double meaning, the religious and mythological meaning, and finally the deep, hidden meaning. *Mele* were a form of oratory, the art held in the highest esteem among the Polynesians. Great orators were men of learning, expert in tradition, history, genealogies and mythology. They performed an important function in the life of the society for through their art they not only entertained, but also educated the community.

All feasts and holidays – times of light-hearted enjoyment – had religious significance. The second part of the festival of *Makahiki*, after the *kapu* had been lifted, was entirely devoted to general merry-making. During this time the great boxing and wrestling tournaments took place, and people gave themselves whole-heartedly to all sorts of sports and games. The interest they had in these pastimes was intensified by their passion for gambling which was very popular and taken very seriously.

Select bibliography

BUCK, PETER H., *Arts and crafts of Hawaii*. Honolulu, 1957.

COX, J. HALLEY, and DAVENPORT, WILLIAM H., *Hawaiian sculpture*. Honolulu, 1974.

COX, J. HALLEY, and STASACK, EDWARD, *Hawaiian petroglyphs*. Honolulu, 1970.

DAY, A. GROVE, *Hawaii and its people*. New York, 1955.

ELLIS, WILLIAM, *Narrative of a tour through Hawaii*. London, 1827.

FEHER, JOSEPH, *Hawaii: a pictorial history*. Honolulu, 1969.

HANDY, E. S. CRAIGHILL, and others, *Ancient Hawaiian civilisation*. Rev. ed. Rutland, Vermont, 1965; reprinted 1970.

II, JOHN PAPA, *Fragments of Hawaiian history*. Honolulu, 1959.

KAMAKAU, SAMUEL M., *Ka poe kahiko: the people of old*. Honolulu, 1964.

LUOMALA, KATHARINE, *Voices on the wind*. Honolulu, 1955.

MALO, DAVID, *Hawaiian antiquities*. Honolulu, 1951.

STEWART, C. S., *Journal of a residence in the Sandwich Islands, during the years 1823, 1824 and 1825*. London, 1828.